EXPLORING JOBS IN THE GIG ECONOMY

GIG JOBS IN
TRANSPORTATION
AND DELIVERY

by A. W. Buckey

BrightP◆int Press

San Diego, CA

BrightPoint Press

© 2023 BrightPoint Press
an imprint of ReferencePoint Press, Inc.
Printed in the United States

For more information, contact:
BrightPoint Press
PO Box 27779
San Diego, CA 92198
www.BrightPointPress.com

LIBRARY OF CONGRESS CATALOGING-IN-PUBLICATION DATA

Names: Buckey, A. W., author.
Title: Gig jobs in transportation and delivery / by A. W. Buckey.
Description: San Diego, CA: BrightPoint Press, [2023] | Series: Exploring
   jobs in the gig economy | Includes bibliographical references and index.
   | Audience: Grades 10-12
Identifiers: LCCN 2022000376 (print) | LCCN 2022000377 (eBook) | ISBN
   9781678203924 (hardcover) | ISBN 9781678203931 (eBook)
Subjects: LCSH: Transportation--Juvenile literature. | Delivery of
   goods--Juvenile literature. | Gig economy--Juvenile literature.
Classification: LCC HE152 .B83 2023 (print) | LCC HE152 (eBook) | DDC
   338.023--dc23/eng/20220325
LC record available at https://lccn.loc.gov/2022000376
LC eBook record available at https://lccn.loc.gov/2022000377

CONTENTS

AT A GLANCE

- Transportation and delivery workers move people and things from one place to another. Their jobs are necessary for business and daily life.

- Gigs are one-time or short-term jobs. In the gig economy, workers make a living by doing gigs for many different customers.

- Rideshare apps such as Uber and Lyft and food delivery apps like Grubhub and DoorDash have greatly increased the number of gig jobs in transportation and delivery.

- Many workers are drawn to the freedom to work multiple jobs, set their own hours, and work alone.

- It can be difficult to make a consistent living from gig work.

- Gig workers do not have workplace benefits like health insurance or paid vacations.

- Large apps have many customers. The future of rideshare and delivery apps is uncertain.

- New technologies like self-driving cars and delivery drones may change the future of delivery and transportation work.

- Many gig workers advocate for better pay and working conditions.

A NIGHT ON THE ROAD

It's after 11 o'clock in a college town. Mamadou is in his sedan, driving a student back to campus. A lot of people are heading to bed. Mamadou holds in a yawn. Maybe he'll get to bed soon too.

The rider in the back asks to listen to music, and Mamadou puts on the college radio station. The fast beat of the song

Rideshare apps can be convenient for people who don't have access to a car or don't want to drive.

gives him a jolt of energy. Mamadou is

usually a night owl, but he's tired from

working long days. Mamadou's a college

student too, studying pre-law and business.

Many food delivery drivers use insulated bags. These bags are designed to help keep food hot longer.

He needs some extra money for books

and living expenses. Mamadou has

always liked driving. So he signed up for

a **rideshare** app. Then, he signed up for another app that lets him deliver food. He can make good money working nights and weekends. And if he needs time off to study, he can stop driving for a while.

Mamadou pulls up to an empty parking space and drops off his rider. The student was quiet and polite. Mamadou swipes for a five-star rating.

Ding! A notification comes in from the delivery app. Someone ordered twenty-five dollars' worth of cookies. They must need a midnight snack. Mamadou looks at the addresses and does some quick math.

Driving to the cookie shop takes five minutes. If the cookies are ready when he gets there, he can be back in his car in two minutes. Then it would take six minutes to get to the apartment, for a total fee of five dollars. He might also get a tip, if he's lucky. Mamadou decides it's worth it and accepts the order. He'll drop off the cookies, and his last drive will be the trip home.

WORKING IN THE GIG ECONOMY

Mamadou is a member of the gig economy. Gigs are temporary jobs that people take on one by one. People have been working in transportation and delivery for

Many gig workers work for more than one company. This helps them maximize the amount of money they make.

thousands of years. For example, some

people carried messages from one place

to another. However, these jobs weren't

gigs in the past. Instead, people worked for one company. They worked as taxi drivers or delivered food for a specific restaurant. In the early 2000s, apps helped change the way these jobs worked. Today, more than one-third of Americans participate in temporary gig jobs. Millions of workers like Mamadou drive passengers or deliver food. Some workers enjoy the freedom and flexibility that gig jobs provide. But these jobs come with many challenges. They can be difficult to sustain long-term.

Many rideshare apps offer different types of rides. Passengers can sometimes request larger cars for more people, nicer cars, or even more eco-friendly rides.

CHAPTER ONE

THE HISTORY OF GIG JOBS IN TRANSPORTATION AND DELIVERY

Transportation means moving people and objects around. Delivery is bringing an object to a certain person or place. All delivery involves transportation of some kind. Cars, planes, boats, and bikes are all types of transportation.

Transportation jobs have a very long history. The first mail delivery service was

Delivery and transportation jobs have existed for a long time. Mail carriers are one example of a non-gig delivery job.

invented more than 2,000 years ago.

Horseback riders in the Persian Empire in

Asia would carry messages from one place

to another.

Gigs have also existed for a long time. The word *gig* is about 300 years old. Starting in the early twentieth century, musicians used the term to refer to performances, but the meaning has expanded over time. Today, people who do gigs are sometimes called freelancers or independent contractors. For example, taxi drivers are often independent contractors. Each customer who hires a taxi pays for his or her own trip. The driver gets paid per car ride. This means that every taxi driver makes a different amount of money each day. People who get set wages from

Taxis were first used in the late 1800s. Now they are common in many cities.

a company are employees. Independent

contractors do not get a guaranteed

minimum wage. They might make lots

of money from a gig or almost none.

However, they have more independence to choose their work.

In the 1970s, many American companies started hiring more independent contractors. Over time, more Americans have started working gig jobs. These jobs are available in many fields. However, getting freelance gigs takes time and effort. Workers need quick, reliable ways to find new customers. In the 1990s, the internet made it easier for people to find gig jobs. For example, the website Craigslist started in 1995. Craigslist has a gigs section for people to find local work. In the 2000s, new smartphone apps made the process easier and more widespread.

THE HISTORY OF GIG JOBS IN TRANSPORTATION

There are many types of transportation jobs. For example, airline pilots, bus drivers, and ferry captains are all transportation

workers. These transportation workers

usually work for a set wage or salary. Before

apps, some transportation work was done

by taxi drivers and car service companies.

Many cities limit the number of people

who can drive taxis. Taxis can be hard to

find in suburban and rural areas. In 2008,

two developers named Travis Kalanick

and Garrett Camp could not find a taxi in

Paris, France. They "wanted to be able to

push a button and get a ride," Kalanick

told the *Atlantic* magazine.[1] In 2009, the

two founded the company Uber. Uber is

Travis Kalanick cofounded Uber in 2009. Kalanick served as Uber's CEO until 2017.

an app-based rideshare company. Users

download the app and enter the address

they want to go to. The app matches them

THE NEW DEAL AND US LABOR LAWS

In the 1930s, the United States went through an economic crisis called the Great Depression. Millions of Americans were jobless during this time. President Franklin Delano Roosevelt helped pass reforms. These reforms were called the New Deal. One law was called the Fair Labor Standards Act (FLSA). This created a minimum wage for jobs. The first minimum wage was twenty-five cents an hour. The FLSA also set a maximum number of hours for a standard workweek.

with a nearby driver. The driver comes to pick them up.

The first Uber ride was in 2010. Five years later, the company had logged a billion car trips. Soon, companies like

Lyft offered apps with similar services.
In order to offer rides, these companies
needed drivers. Uber and Lyft expanded the
number of people who could do rideshare
work. People could sign up quickly. They
could also start working in cars they already
owned. Rideshare driver Brett Helling points
out, "The signup process is pretty simple
and takes just a few minutes."[2] Usually,
rideshare drivers can start working within a
week of signing up with an app.

THE HISTORY OF DELIVERY GIG JOBS

Takeout and food delivery became popular
in the United States in the 1950s. Before the

internet, customers would order their food by phone. In the 1990s, some restaurants started putting menus online. In 1995, a California company called World Wide Waiter collected many restaurant menus on the same website. A similar company called Seamless launched in 1999. Grubhub started in 2004. Both Seamless and Grubhub expanded to smartphone apps.

Before food delivery apps, restaurants would hire their own delivery workers. These delivery workers did not pick up gigs. Instead, they worked for just one restaurant. They got hourly wages. As delivery apps

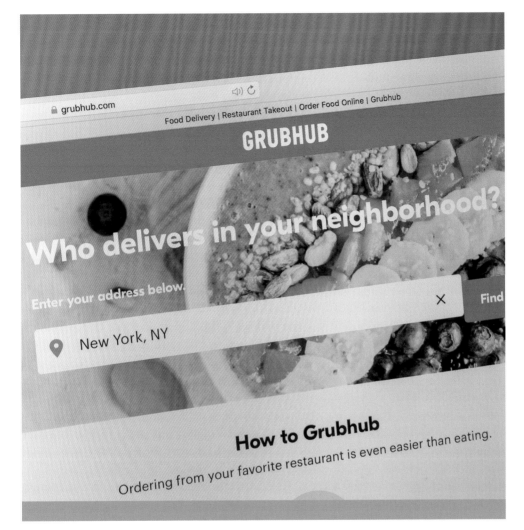

Grubhub first started in Chicago, Illinois, before expanding to the rest of the United States. The company launched its first app in 2009.

grew, many more restaurants began offering

delivery. The apps started hiring their own

delivery workers. These food delivery

workers were independent contractors.

Food delivery started to become a gig job.

In 2013, Seamless and Grubhub merged.

By 2021, Grubhub offered food from more

than 300,000 US restaurants. There are

other food delivery companies such as

Deliveroo and DoorDash. Even Uber has a food delivery wing called Uber Eats.

These apps created many new jobs. According to the ADP Research Institute, the number of gig workers grew 15 percent between 2010 and 2020. In 2020, about 1.5 million workers drove for Uber and Lyft in the United States. In 2021, DoorDash said it had hired almost 2 million workers worldwide in less than a year. Many of these workers are men. But the number of women increased during the COVID-19 pandemic. Delivery workers tend to be older, married, and parents.

CHAPTER TWO

WORKING A GIG JOB IN TRANSPORTATION AND DELIVERY

Gig workers in rideshare and food delivery often work for many companies. Some workers split their time between rideshare and delivery work.

RIDESHARE JOBS

Rideshare workers drive customers in their cars. Apps make it possible for drivers and

Gig workers often enjoy the flexibility of their jobs.

customers to find each other. A customer

downloads the company's smartphone

app. The app finds the customer's location.

Apps like Uber or Lyft increase prices for rides if there aren't many drivers available. This practice is called surge pricing.

The app tracks the locations of drivers logged in to work too. The app matches customers who want rides with nearby drivers. A driver gets a notification with the customer's location. The driver can decide whether to accept the ride. Rideshare apps calculate the driver's **fare** ahead of time. This fare affects the driver's decision. Drivers want well-paying rides. Uber and Lyft are two very popular rideshare apps. Others, like Waze Carpool, let people form groups to share rides.

Rideshare drivers can work for many apps at the same time. Mike is a delivery driver who makes videos under the name Your Driver Mike. "I want you to drive on as many apps as you can," Mike tells drivers.[3] This way, drivers have access to more customers. Different apps offer different bonuses for drivers. For example, Lyft offers weekly scheduled bonuses to drivers. Uber offers a sign-up bonus to new drivers.

FOOD DELIVERY JOBS

Food delivery apps work by connecting restaurants, customers, and delivery people. First, restaurants decide to work

INTERNATIONAL GIG JOBS

Many of the largest app service companies, like Uber and Amazon, are based in the United States. But gig jobs exist in many countries. Uber operated in more than seventy countries and territories as of 2021. Some apps are based outside the United States. Canada's most popular online delivery app is called SkipTheDishes. In India, the rideshare service Ola Cabs is popular.

with a food delivery app like Grubhub. The apps charge restaurants in a few different ways. They take 20 to 30 percent of the money from each online order. So, if a customer orders a twenty-dollar dinner, a delivery app might take four dollars. The apps also charge the restaurant other fees. For example, Grubhub gives each restaurant a phone number for orders. Until August 2021, Grubhub charged the restaurant for customer calls to the number, even when orders were not placed.

In exchange, apps publish the restaurant's menu online. Delivery apps track workers' locations like rideshare apps. When an order comes in, the app sends it to nearby workers. Each worker can accept or reject the order. The person who accepts the order first gets the job. That worker picks up the food and drops it off. Food delivery workers drive in many parts of the country. But workers can use different types of transportation. In New York City, many delivery workers use bikes.

There are also apps for groceries and other food deliveries. Instacart workers shop at grocery stores and deliver the food to customers. The company Gopuff offers

Some food delivery apps allow people to deliver food by foot or bike. This can be faster for workers in some cities.

convenience store snacks and groceries.

Postmates, owned by Uber, combines all

these types of deliveries. Users can order

from restaurants or stores. They can order

non-grocery items like paper towels or

pet food.

PACKAGE DELIVERY JOBS

Companies depend on delivery services to

send goods to customers. Apps like Shipt

and Roadie connect businesses to drivers.

These drivers pick up items at a business

and drop them off at a customer's address.

This is called last-mile delivery.

Amazon is the biggest shopping

website in the United States. It sold almost

$400 billion worth of products in 2020.

The company offers a paid service called

Amazon Prime. Amazon Prime customers

TIPPING GIG WORKERS

A tip is an extra payment for a service. Customers decide whether to tip and what the tip amount is. In the United States, it's traditional to tip for car rides and food delivery. A typical tip for a ride or food delivery is 15 to 20 percent of the cost. Many smartphone apps allow customers to add a tip online. Package delivery work is traditionally untipped. So is shipping and **freight** work.

get one-day shipping on many items. In 2019, 66.4 million US households had an Amazon Prime subscription. Amazon must be ready to ship items on very short notice. The company does this by keeping items at warehouses called fulfillment centers.

Amazon offered Amazon Flex jobs in more than fifty cities as of 2021.

There are 110 of these warehouses in the United States. The company also sends items to smaller warehouses called sortation centers. Amazon has a big need for last-mile delivery. Traditional delivery companies like UPS do some of that work. But Amazon saves money when it hires its own delivery workers.

This is why the company has a gig delivery service called Amazon Flex. Amazon Flex workers pick up orders from fulfillment and sortation centers. They get packages for many customers at the same time. This job is easiest for workers who live near fulfillment centers. "If you happen to live closer to the delivery station, I think it's definitely worth doing," Amazon Flex worker Quan Tsang told CNBC.[4]

Online shopping boomed during the COVID-19 pandemic. This greatly increased the need for delivery drivers.

MOVING, SHIPPING, AND FREIGHT JOBS

There are apps like Dolly, Lugg, and GoShare for people who own trucks or vans. People who can lift heavy items can also sign up to work with the apps. Workers on these apps can do tasks like helping someone move furniture. They can also work with businesses to deliver large items.

There are many different kinds of delivery. For example, grocery stores get their products delivered in large shipments. Often, these products come from all around the world. Businesses depend on international transport and delivery of huge amounts of items. This kind of transportation is called shipping and freight. Some apps are looking to make shipping and freight a bigger part of the gig economy. Uber and Amazon both have freight apps. They are called Uber Freight and Amazon Relay. They match large shipments with long-distance truck drivers.

CHAPTER THREE

PROS AND CONS OF GIG JOBS IN TRANSPORTATION AND DELIVERY

Gig jobs have upsides and downsides. Many workers like to work independently. They enjoy setting their own hours. But independent contractors don't have a lot of job security. It can also be difficult to make money doing gig work. Demand for service from the apps can change without much notice for workers.

During the COVID-19 pandemic, many restaurants relied on delivery to stay open. This created more work for delivery workers.

SELF-EMPLOYMENT

Job hunting can be a long and difficult

process. But it is usually easy to sign up

for gig jobs. For example, Kristina Lynn

is an Instacart shopper. After applying to

Many grocery delivery services grew quickly during the COVID-19 pandemic. Online grocery orders tripled between 2019 and 2021.

work with the company, she had to pass

a background check. Then, she got a

debit card from the company. Lynn had

to watch a few training videos and take

some quizzes. Then, she was ready to start working. The process took only a few days. Lynn did not have to go through an interview process. She was also free to do other jobs. However, many full-time jobs offer benefits such as health insurance and paid sick days. Gig workers do not usually get these benefits.

FLEXIBLE HOURS

Gig workers can set their own work hours. This helps people plan around responsibilities like childcare. Workers can also adjust their hours as needed. They can work more when they need more money.

They may work less when they have other things to do.

Gig workers can also choose to accept or turn down orders. This flexibility helps workers make more money in less time. Workers try to find orders that pay the most for the least time spent. "I decline offers that are taking me too far and it's going to take me too long to deliver," DoorDasher Virginia Blanchard explains.[5] However, apps try to limit this flexibility. They deactivate workers who refuse a lot of offers. Deactivation is when the app stops letting a worker log in. It's similar to getting fired.

Flexible hours also mean flexible pay.

Every driver makes a different amount

of money. And the person has to pay for

his or her own expenses like oil changes

Sometimes drivers only have to wait a few minutes for a new request, but other times they need to wait much longer.

and car washes. Some gig workers

spend more than others on expenses. For

example, some rideshare drivers have large,

expensive cars. They pay more for the cars, but they can charge higher fees for rides.

No one knows exactly what the typical wage for a gig transportation or delivery worker is. In New York City in 2021, food delivery drivers made around twelve dollars an hour. A study by Cornell University estimated that rideshare drivers in Seattle, Washington, made around twenty-three dollars an hour. The website Ridester, however, gives a rate of closer to ten dollars an hour in some cities.

A living wage is the amount of money needed for things like food and shelter.

In 2020, Massachusetts Institute of Technology's (MIT) living wage calculator said that the US living wage for a family of four was $16.54. According to Ridester, delivery and transportation workers do not make a living wage for a family. According to the Cornell study, they do.

The Cornell study's estimate was higher partly because it measured work time differently. The researchers decided that gig workers were only "at work" when they were driving customers or about to pick someone up. The study raises an important question. How much of a gig worker's day

Someone who works for a restaurant may have to do other tasks between deliveries. A gig worker does not.

is actually work? A pizza delivery driver, for

example, gets paid for the time he spends

waiting for orders to come in. But if a gig

worker waits for half an hour, that time is

unpaid. Neither person is actively working

between new orders. The hourly worker must work until his shift ends. The gig worker can work for as long he wants.

CUSTOMER CONTACT

Some gig drivers like being able to work directly with customers. Rideshare driver Al Castillo enjoys meeting the different people who get in his car. Gig workers can rate customers on their behavior on some apps. In exchange, customers rate their drivers and workers. Both workers and customers can report **harassment** and abuse. However, customers and workers say that apps often don't take complaints seriously.

Ratings are a way drivers and customers can warn other users about rude or unsafe behavior.

Sometimes, it can be difficult to work without support from other workers. Gig workers may find themselves alone in tricky situations. Amazon Flex driver Jonathan has felt unsafe making deliveries. He worries that people will see him approach a house

RACE, CUSTOMERS, AND RIDESHARE APPS

There is a history of racial discrimination in the transportation business. A 2000 study showed that in many cities taxi drivers were much less likely to stop for Black passengers. Some Black people hoped that rideshare apps would help reduce this discrimination. They thought it might be easier to find a ride on an app instead of in person. However, a 2016 study found that Black customers in Seattle waited longer for rides on the apps. In Boston, Massachusetts, Black customers who ordered rideshares were more likely to be canceled on.

and assume he is a criminal. Someone might attack him or call the police on him. To avoid this, Jonathan ordered himself a sweatshirt that says "Amazon Flex." But he thinks the company should pay for worker uniforms. "I think . . . the least they could do is give us something that would make it a little bit safer," Jonathan told CNBC.[6]

Apps can offer some protections to workers. For example, taxi drivers have to deal with customers who leave their cars without paying. But apps like Uber store customers' credit card information.

INDEPENDENT WORK LIFE

Gig workers are not stuck in one place all day. They get to move around and visit new places. But travel has downsides too. One ongoing problem for workers is lack of bathroom access. Many delivery workers say that the restaurants they deliver for won't let them use the bathroom. One group of gig workers helped fix the problem. In 2020, they made a smartphone app called Whizz. It has a map with locations of usable bathrooms.

Delivery and transportation jobs are some of the more dangerous jobs in the United States. In 2018, taxi driving ranked seventeenth on a US government list of the most dangerous jobs. Delivery jobs ranked seventh. Some of the dangers come from the risks of driving or biking in urban areas. Workers can also be robbed. They work alone and carry valuable objects

There are risks to delivery or transportation work. Some organizations offer workers tips and suggestions to try to stay safe.

like smartphones. This makes them good

targets for thieves. A survey of New York

City delivery workers found that more than

half had been robbed. About 30 percent

had been physically attacked.

CHAPTER FOUR

THE FUTURE OF GIG JOBS IN TRANSPORTATION AND DELIVERY

Uber and Lyft did not invent rideshare apps. But they were the first rideshare apps to become popular. Now, rideshare and delivery apps are all over the world. Delivery apps are part of daily life. People rely on them to fill many needs. But even as it grows, the gig economy may not be built to last.

As apps grow, some places like airports have specific spaces set aside for gig workers.

WILL THE GIG BUBBLE BURST?

Many app companies grew thanks to

venture capital funding. Venture capital

firms find companies that they think have

good ideas. They give those companies

large amounts of money. In exchange,

the firms own part of the companies.

Venture capitalists bet on companies they think will grow. For example, Uber had received $10 billion in venture capital money by 2015. This money helped it hire drivers and make advertisements. At first, Uber and other apps kept their prices low. This helped them get as many customers as possible.

By 2020, Uber's yearly revenue was more than $11 billion. But the company did not make a **profit**. The company spent more than it took in. In fact, it lost more than $6 billion that year. Grubhub lost more than $155 million in 2020. DoorDash

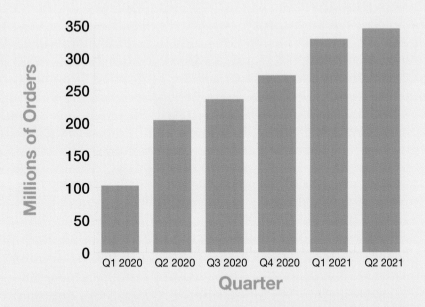

TOTAL DOORDASH ORDERS DURING THE COVID-19 PANDEMIC

Source: Jackie Davalos, "DoorDash Falls Amid Steep Costs to Sustain Pandemic Growth," Bloomberg, August 21, 2021. www.bloomberg.com.

The COVID-19 pandemic caused many people to turn to delivery instead of going out to eat. The number of DoorDash orders increased as restaurants closed indoor dining.

lost $461 million. These huge losses are

common for rideshare and delivery apps.

Venture capital firms do not want to fund

these businesses forever. In order to

survive, apps have to find a way to make

a profit.

The COVID-19 pandemic was a crisis

point for many food delivery apps. They

had more customers than ever. But they

were still losing money. "The question that companies like DoorDash and Uber Eats are now asking internally is can we make money delivering food alone?" explains tech reporter Preetika Rana. "And I think that the companies . . . have come up with a short answer for that, which is no."[7] Now, apps are looking for ways to make more money. One possible solution is expanding deliveries. The apps want to convince people to order from restaurants and other stores at the same time. They suggest extra items to order. If a customer buys more, workers and companies get more money.

Rideshare companies are optimistic that they can grow enough to make money. The company Lyft reported a profit in the second part of 2021. It is worried about a driver shortage, however. Some business experts argue that companies like Uber overestimate how much money they make. The future of these apps is still uncertain.

NEW TRANSPORTATION TECHNOLOGIES

Several companies are experimenting with non-human transportation and delivery. Domino's is the world's largest pizza company. The company hires its own delivery drivers. In 2021, Domino's began

AMAZON DRONES

Amazon is starting to deliver some packages by drone. Its drone delivery service is called Prime Air. In 2020, the US government gave Amazon permission to start using these drones. Amazon's goal is to deliver packages to customers in thirty minutes instead of one day. The drones are small. They can carry packages that weigh 5 pounds (2.3 kg) or less. They fly using propellers and can travel 15 miles (24.1 km).

testing a self-driving delivery car in Houston, Texas. The car drives to a customer's home. The customer opens the car door with an access code. Customers take out the pizza themselves. If other companies get this technology, there could be fewer food delivery jobs. But Domino's does not expect

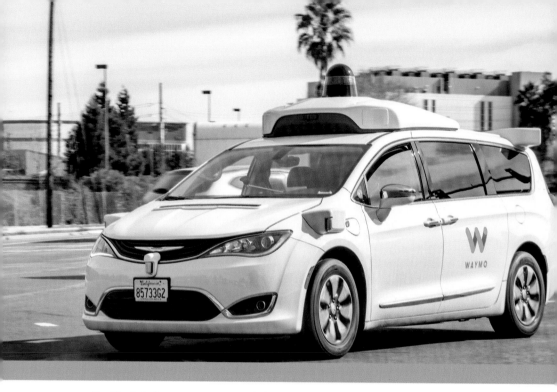

Self-driving cars use things like sensors, maps, and lasers to navigate safely. However, the cars can be confused when there is something unexpected on the road.

to replace all delivery workers. It wants to

combine drivers with self-driving delivery.

In Phoenix, Arizona, a service named

Waymo offers robot taxis. The tech

company Alphabet is behind Waymo.

Alphabet also owns Google. Waymo has

its own app for requesting rides. Waymo

vans do not have human drivers. However,

some vans still have humans on board

for emergencies. Waymo believes that

its technology can help reduce driving

accidents. However, self-driving car

technology is still new. Many people are

nervous about using these cars before all

errors are fixed.

TRANSPORTATION AND DELIVERY WORKERS LOOK AHEAD

If apps cannot make money, they will fail.

Transportation and delivery workers would

have to find new jobs. As technology

Gig workers have used strikes to protest pay, benefits, or working conditions. Organizations from other industries will sometimes join in support.

changes, gig workers will have to adjust.

But many workers are more concerned

about the present than the future. Gig

transportation and delivery jobs have a

high turnover rate. This means that people

often do not stay in these jobs for very long.

Low pay is a major factor. In July 2021, DoorDash delivery workers held a one-day strike to protest low pay. In 2020, the average DoorDash order cost the customer thirty-six dollars. DoorDash generally pays workers between two dollars and ten dollars per order. This does not include tips. In addition, delivery workers could not see their tips before accepting orders. "I've declined so many orders because they've been $2," DoorDasher Denise Small explained on TikTok.[8]

Transportation and delivery workers have gotten together to share how they believe the business should work. The International Transport Workers' Federation (ITF), for example, has rules it says app-based businesses should follow. The ITF says that workers should be paid a living wage. They should get benefits like health insurance.

At the beginning of the COVID-19 pandemic, delivery and transportation gig workers were essential workers. They continued driving and delivering during widespread lockdowns. Many gig workers remember the stress and uncertainty of that time. "When the city was shut down, we were the ones running the restaurants, we were carrying that industry on our backs,"

New York City delivery worker Williams Sian

told reporters.[9] Sian was making a point

about the importance of his work. Some

gig workers want to drive and deliver as

employees, not independent contractors. In

LOS DELIVERISTAS UNIDOS

Many delivery workers in New York City
are immigrants from other countries. Los
Deliveristas Unidos is a group for New York
delivery workers. The group tries to improve
working conditions. Los Deliveristas Unidos
scored a victory in September 2021. New York
City passed a law to improve conditions for
delivery workers. The bill guarantees bathroom
access to workers, for example. It also lets
workers refuse to make long delivery trips.

2020 and 2021, there was a legal battle in California over gig workers. The companies behind major gig apps helped pass a law that said rideshare drivers couldn't be employees. This law passed in 2020, but many protested it. In 2021, a California judge said that the law wasn't valid. This legal fight is one example of the debate over how well the gig economy works.

Transportation and delivery jobs existed before apps. These jobs will continue to be important for society. But society has to figure out if the gig economy is what's best for customers and workers.

In May 2019, protesters gathered in front of Uber's headquarters. They raised concerns about cutbacks on bonuses, the large number of drivers, and unfair deactivations.

GLOSSARY

fare

money paid for a ride in a car or other mode of transportation

freight

transportation of large amounts of goods or the goods themselves

harassment

bullying and abusive treatment, such as insults or unwanted touching

profit

when a business earns more money than it spends

revenue

the incoming money for a business

rideshare

a paid trip in a private car or vehicle

venture capital

investment in a new company to help it grow

SOURCE NOTES

CHAPTER ONE: THE HISTORY OF GIG JOBS IN TRANSPORTATION AND DELIVERY

1. Quoted in Megan McArdle, "Why You Can't Get a Taxi," *Atlantic*, May 2012. www.theatlantic.com.

2. Brett Helling, "Become an Uber Driver: Requirements & Signup," *Ridester*, September 23, 2021. www.ridester.com.

CHAPTER TWO: WORKING A GIG JOB IN TRANSPORTATION AND DELIVERY

3. Your Driver Mike, "Driving for Multiple Delivery Apps (Step-by-Step Strategy)," *YouTube*, August 23, 2020. www.youtube.com.

4. Quoted in "What It's Like to Be an Amazon Flex Delivery Driver," *CNBC*, June 19, 2019. www.youtube.com.

CHAPTER THREE: PROS AND CONS OF GIG JOBS IN TRANSPORTATION AND DELIVERY

5. Quoted in Ahmed Ali Akbar, "Who's Driving Whom?" *Land of the Giants*, July 6, 2021. www.eater.com.

6. Quoted in "What It's Like to Be an Amazon Flex Delivery Driver."

CHAPTER FOUR: THE FUTURE OF GIG JOBS IN TRANSPORTATION AND DELIVERY

7. Quoted in David Brown, "Can Food Apps Ever Deliver Profits?" *Food Delivery Wars*, June 21, 2021. https://wondery.com/shows/Business-Wars.

8. Quoted in Josie Fischels, "Why DoorDash Drivers Are on Strike," *NPR*, July 31, 2021. www.npr.org.

9. Quoted in Claudia Irizarry Aponte and Josefa Velasquez, "NYC Delivery Workers Band to Demand Better Treatment. Will New York Listen to Los Deliveristas Unidos?" *The City*, December 6, 2020. www.thecity.nyc.

FOR FURTHER RESEARCH

BOOKS

Heidi Ayarbe, *Gig Jobs in High-Tech*. San Diego, CA: BrightPoint Press, 2023.

Kerry Dinmont, *Frontline Workers During COVID-19*. San Diego, CA: BrightPoint Press, 2021.

Bridey Heing, *The Gig Economy*. New York: Greenhaven Publishing, 2021.

INTERNET SOURCES

"Eater Partners with Recode for Land of the Giants: Delivery Wars," *Eater*, June 15, 2021. www.eater.com.

Maria Figueroa et al., "Essential but Unprotected: App-Based Food Couriers in New York City," *Los Deliveristas Unidos*, n.d. https://losdeliveristasunidos.org.

Alyse Whitney, "What It's Really Like to Be an Instacart Shopper," *Bon Appétit*, September 26, 2017. www.bonappetit.com.

WEBSITES

International Transport Workers' Federation
www.itfglobal.org

The International Transport Workers' Federation is an organization that works for better pay and conditions for transport workers. It publishes research and news on transportation gig workers.

Ridester
www.ridester.com

Founded by rideshare driver Brett Helling, Ridester is a website that helps people navigate gig jobs in transportation and delivery.

The State of Gig Work in 2021
www.pewresearch.org/internet/2021/12/08/the-state-of-gig -work-in-2021

The Pew Research Center is a group that provides information on issues. Their research on the gig economy evaluates benefits, drawbacks, and issues facing gig workers.

INDEX

IMAGE CREDITS

ABOUT THE AUTHOR

A. W. Buckey is a writer living in Brooklyn, New York.